Spare Moments

Dedicated to the Memory of
Wyn & Nellie

Wyndham Albert Williams (1915 - 1967)

Wyndham Albert Williams was born in Brynamman, one of three children of miner William Williams and his wife, Martha. Showing promise from an early age, he won a place at Amman Valley Grammar School and matriculated at only 15.

He took up employment as Relieving Officer in Ammanford but continued his interests of singing in the Chapel choir, playing the mandolin, zither and guitar, and performing in "Go as you please" events.

In 1937 he married Nellie Brooks and proved a devoted husband and later, a loving father to six children. He and Nellie moved to Whitland, Wyndham working as Relieving Officer and Registrar of Births, Deaths and Marriages. Both partners were popular members of the community and were frequent performers at the "Welcome Home" concerts, keeping up morale; Wyndham playing the mandolin, guitar, ukelele, or banjo, and singing along with Nellie to all sorts of songs including those of George Formby.

In 1942 Wyndham was called up and became a member of the Royal Army Co., and later the 4th Royal Tank Regiment. As a soldier his cheerful manner and gift for poetry made him very popular among his fellow comrades. His first surviving poem dates from 1934 and concerns war in Abyssinia. This output increased rapidly as a result of his personal experiences in battle. For his immense bravery and devotion to duty he was decorated with the Croix de Guerre with Bronze Star by General de Gaulle, and the Commander in Chief's Certificate of Gallantry in the field.

In 1946 he returned to civilian life, and his profession in Whitland. Continuing to help everyone he could, he was a popular and very well known member of the community. His entertaining and enjoyment of life continued, with him

becoming a Scout Master, a Sunday School Teacher, a member of the British Legion, the RAOB, as well as one of a small number of extremely keen river fishermen. In all these he was enthusiastically supported by Nellie.

He was troubled by heart problems from the mid 1950's, but refused to let up on his activities, and in 1967 died of a massive heart attack. His loss was felt not only by his wife and five living children, but by his many friends. To this day, the younger members of his family are still referred to locally as relatives of "Williams the Registrar".

Spare Moments

Wyn Williams

Gronw Publications

Gronw Publications
Stoneleigh
Thornberry Gardens
Ludchurch
Narberth
Pembrokeshire
SA67 8JQ

First published in 2005
© Wyn Williams 2005
All rights reserved

ISBN 1 902638 64 6

Cover design by Lucy Llewellyn
Printed and bound by Dinefwr Press, Llandybïe, Wales

British Library cataloguing in publication data

A cataloguing record for this book is available from the British Library

This book is sold subject to the condition that it shall not by way of trade or otherwise be circulated without the publisher's prior consent in any form of binding or cover other than that in which it is published and without a similar condition including the condition being imposed on the subsequent purchaser

Contents

The First Aggression (Abyssinia)	1
When Warmonger?	2
Higham Heath Camp	4
Squadron Leaders, Past & Present	
1. Major Haines	7
2. Captain Veal	10
3. Major Pickering	11
4. Major Lovibond	12
Opportunity	14
Ambition	15
The Gunner's Prayer	16
Life is but a Day	17
My Wedding Anniversary 1944	18
A Moonlight Ramble	19
Chrysanthemum	20
In Memory of Lieut. Eric Jones	22
Peace	23
To My Son	25
A Ballad of Wester Kappeln	30
Little Man, What Now?	32
Nelly	34
Captain Thorne, HQ Squadron	35
Behold, The Man	38
Above Costozza	39
Dear Dad (or The Fatigue Squad)	40
Sergeant Major	41
Glory	43
To 'Dally' the Canteen Girl	45

The Victory Parade, Trieste	46
To a Nightingale	49
Squadron Leaders, Past & Present (2)	
Major Reed, MC	51
To My Bed	53
The Prisoner of Buchenwald	55
The London Victory Parade	59
Churchill	62
To My Boots	64
Rocky Knight	66
To Taffy Ryan on his Wedding	69
In Memory of Len Hill	71
The Miner's Death	73
In Memory of Alderman T L Phillips	75
The Wedding of G Williams & Eileen 'Clyde Bank'	77
The Dairies' Pin-Up Girl	80
To 'Benji the Post'	83
The Wedding of Eddie Davies & Marion Morgan	87

To the memory of Wyn & Nellie

The First Aggression (Abyssinia)

They called thee emperor but yesterday,
And hailed thee with the greeting of a friend,
And yet, when Rome decreed thy reign should end,
They, like the Levite, turned the other way.
Mighty thy faith, thy courage mightier aye,
Than theirs, who, feigning deafness, let thee fend
For thine own self, when, wounded thou didst rend
Their ears with pleas for help. How deaf were they
Who in thine hour of need did thee forsake.
What fate! Grim irony, today behold,
They who once fed the guns, wherewith to take
Thy kingdom from thee, now would feign enfold
Thy shame with pity. Grant that God, may make,
Not even as their shame, their pity – cold.

Brynamman, 1934

When Warmonger?

When will ye learn that talk of war
Is but the folly of the wise,
When will this lust for power cease
To blind thine eyes?

Hast thou no nobler aim in life,
Than but to covet for thyself,
The doubtful blessing of a victor's
Fame and pelf?

Shall each re-arming impulse sway
The future of the nation's youth?
Must vain desire warp thy reasoning
From the truth?

That they who live by might of arms
By that same power perish must,
And all the glory of their strength
Be brought to dust.

What of our women? These the hope
Of generations yet unborn,
Shall they in motherhoods dark hour
Be left forlorn?

What of our babes? From out the slums
Of our great cities comes their cry,
"Give us each day our daily bread
Or else we die."

And dost thou give them all to eat?
Vain hope – thou with the selfsame breath,
Dost clamour for more guns wherewith
To hasten death.

Strength is thy God, yet know ye not,
That save when used to help the poor,
Thy might is but the useless talent
Of a boor.

The crown of life is not for those
Who but the claims of self observe,
They only win it who have learnt
The way to serve.

I yearn to greet a brighter dawn,
When man the might of peace shall prove,
And seek his destiny in deeds
Of selfless love.

Whitland, 14th December 1938

Higham Heath Camp

I'll sing for you a soldier's tale,
(Of special interest to each male)
It's all about a woody dale,
Called Little Higham.

It's famous as a soldiers' camp.
(And since the atmosphere's not damp)
The sale of beer is a ramp
In Little Higham.

Some say it is a beauty spot,
But this I think is sheer rot,
I've seen some sights, but it was not
Down Little Higham.

Few are the ladies that we find,
And these are of the stuck-up kind,
They never stop to look behind,
These belles of Higham.

Do we like women? No, not much,
And this place lacks the female touch,
It's quite ideal for monks and such
In Little Higham.

The squadron cooks here, all they do
Is have their bony chests tattooed
With saucy women in the nude
To shock all Higham.

They dish their dinners up in pails,
Just like they do in 'Eyetie' jails
No wonder troopers bite their nails
At camp in Higham.

The soldiers hunt for food like cats,
They're even keener than the rats,
Some are reduced to chewing mats
At camp in Higham.

The tripping ropes between each tent,
The miles of wire entanglement,
I'll rue each blinking hour I spent
At Little Higham.

We have to sign for everythin'
For every tank and every pin,
You'll never guess the state we're in
At Little Higham.

The nightly Squadron Orders too,
They're all too long – I'm telling you
They'd stretch right down to Timbuctoo
From Little Higham.

We haven't got no blinkin' tanks,
This army must be run by cranks,
But does it worry us? No thanks
Not down in Higham.

We're being led a merry chase,
It's all to save the army's face,
For, barring Dartmoor, there's no place
Like Little Higham.

Still, Friday is the biggest day,
At least that's what the fellows say,
For that is when they draw their pay
At camp in Higham.

But when they're paid! Why, in these camps,
Of all the rotten played-out ramps,
There's nowt to spend it on, save stamps,
In Little Higham.

We hard-worked troops are starving still,
And since we all go through the mill,
We've nearly had more than our fill
Of Little Higham.

So if old Jerry has a bomb,
I hope he'll hurry up and come,
And drop the blighter, when we're gone
On Little Higham.

Higham Heath, Bury St. Edmunds, June 1943

Squadron Leaders, Past & Present

1. Major Haines

'Twas in '42, the year of our Lord,
In the reign of good King George,
Days when the homes of England rang
With the fame of Alamein gorge.
When Monty's name was a household word,
As Nelson's once had been,
And the flower of our country pledged their all
For their nation, king and queen.

Those, my friends, were the days when we,
Fresh from the tang of the Scottish hills,
Moved with the hundred and forty-fourth,
(Complete with blancho, polish and frills,)
Moved right down to the sunny south,
Down to the south of the sunny plains,
Led by the hero of this my tale,
To whit, the Major, Donald 'Tash' Haines.

Tall was he and long of limb,
In the Abraham Lincoln style,
With a characteristic, loping gait,
Which singled him out a mile,
Neat and slim in every line,
At least from what I could see,
And I guess if you'd looked at him sideways,
You'd have called him an absentee.

He was stately and tall in his bearing,
As befits a fellow with cash,
But some friend, in an unguarded moment, prevailed
Upon him to grow a moustache.
'Twas not of the measly two-inch type,
That you meet every day on the street,
But this was a tash to be proud of,
And it measured just under two feet.

It covered the whole of his long upper lip,
One foot each side of his nose,
While deep in the undergrowth somewhere,
The tip of his nozzle reposed.
In the centre, 'twas cut fine and thinly,
While it broadened right out at the ends,
'Twas a source of real envy to most of us chaps,
And the pride and the joy of his friends.

I find we associate sometimes,
Man's deeds with his habits and traits,
For 'tis said that old Monty was picking his nose
When he stormed the Sicilian straits,
But Donald did nothing so common,
And if things didn't come up to scratch,
You would know what kind of a mood he was in,
By watching him tug his moustache.

'Tis thus that I like to remember
That first squadron leader of mine,
For though later ones have been clever,
The size of their tashes decline.
So here's to the first, may the days of his life
Reach beyond the specified span,
May I, who so envied that tash that was his
Live to grow one as big if I can.

Bury St. Edmunds, 6th January 1944

2. In Memory of Captain Veal, Medical Officer, 144 RAC Killed at Noyers, France, in July 1944, While Recovering Wounded Troops

A man of sacrifice has passed away,
In his life's morning, 'neath a foreign sun.
The promise of the years to come – undone,
Like a shorn seedling in the warm noonday.
Recall in grateful memory all who may,
Find cause to bless some service that was done,
'Neath shell and fire of the loathed Hun,
By him who gave his all for such as they.
I shall not rest me, neither shall this day
Shed its last rays upon me, ere this one,
Who bore his love for all, malice for none,
Shall be avenged. Of him in truth it may,
Be writ in reverence upon his grave,
"Others he saved; himself he could not save."

Goneville-Le-Mallet, France, August 1944

3. In Memory of Major Pickering, Killed at Noyers

To live courageously, when each new dawn,
Renews the challenge of their destiny,
Is but a common lot of those who weave,
The hackneyed pattern of life's tapestry.

To die courageously, while in their youth,
And not decry the unexpected blow,
Which made an end of all tomorrow's hopes,
Calls for a courage only few can know.

Yet, such a one I knew, who, in his prime,
Was called upon to suffer and to die,
Whose courage in the certainty of death
Set an example for such men as I.

And in the days to come, should adverse tides
Sweep o'er me, and engulf my peaceful way,
I'll face whatever fickle fate may send,
With courage he bequeathed to me today.

Noyers, France, 16th July 1944

4. In Memory of Major Lovibond, Killed at Noyers

No Tom, the easy path was not for you,
You fretted at the thought that you must stay,
Away from the danger. 'Twas the will to lead
Your boys in battle brought you death today.

You had the choice, aye Tom you had to beg
To be allowed to follow your own heart,
That selfless heart which said, "Where my boys are,
And where death threatens, I must do my part."

How oft have others had this selfsame choice,
To stay behind and watch as from afar
The tide of battle, or to risk their all,
In one triumphant hazard in the war.

And lacking that self-sacrificing will
To go where conscious leads – or smooth, or rough,
Have chosen safety, saying to themselves,
"When I am called for will be soon enough."

Ah me, tomorrow soon will come again,
But who will volunteer in your stead,
To lead us, when so few have come before,
And with true leadership avenge our dead?

Enough. Let the example which you gave
Of sacrifice for others lend to me,
The strength to do the same, that this my life,
May be a living requiem for thee.

Noyers, France, 17th July 1944

Opportunity

Despise not opportunity my son,
But make of it a stepping stone whereby
All those ideals which you have placed so high,
May be accomplished ere your race is run.
The heights of glory which great men have won,
Were not the product of a single try
At Fortune's wheel – no moment passed them by,
But that it offered scope for something done.
They sought the vision of their goal like men,
Who know that opportunities await,
The man who breasts each stubborn tide, and then
Still struggles on in spite of adverse fate.
Dame Fortune will not offer you again,
The prize lost opportunities create.

Tilly-sur-Sulles, France, 10th July 1944

Ambition

Life is a feast, whereof we all partake,
All men their portion have – some more, some less
Than that which God has planned, so that success
In life may be the end which all can make.
Men, ever selfish from their neighbours take,
What lust has coveted in sinfulness,
Blind to their many faults their eyes, no less
Their ears, deaf to the call of hearts they break.
Greed is the foremost rung on which they start
Scaling to seek some personal gain, and oft
Striving for worldly eminence, the part
Which someone else should play, they steal.
How soft falls on their ears the pleading of some heart
They crushed beneath their feet to climb aloft.

Tilly-sur-Sulles, France, 28th July 1944

The Gunner's Prayer

Oh God, who in thy mercy gavest man,
In this world's Genesis, life-giving breath,
And seest here today how I, thy son
Have now usurped the dreadful power of death,
I pray that in thy mercy, Lord, thine eyes
Will see beyond my seeming act of sin,
And find my motives to be pure, oh Lord,
My hope of thy salvation lies therein.

I seek but to destroy that which denies,
To me, the right to love and follow thee,
And seeks to make thy gospel but a myth,
And thee a legend in life's history.
I cannot with impunity stand by,
While foes who love not thee enthrone the wrong,
And torture those thy sons, who in despair,
Cry out to heaven, "How long, oh Lord, how long?"

Make straight my aim, oh Lord, nor let me cease
To fire my guns, till they shall cry for peace.

Goneville Le Mallet, France, 2nd August 1944

Life is but a Day

Short is our day from sunrise to its close.
Oft-times obscuring clouds befog our way.
Sweet is the dawn of childhood, and each day
Fairer the world wherein we live. No foes
Darken our path till noonday brings its woes
In shattered dreams, and childhood's roundelay
Takes on a graver note, that we may play
To nobler tune life's anthem to its close.
Anon comes evening – dread of the unknown
Passions unleashed within, like dormant fires
Brings in its train a torment of its own –
The hell-bred torment of unquenched desires.
Yet he who seeks may find the greater light,
Ere life is lost in death, and day in night.

Antwerp, Belgium, October 1944

My Wedding Anniversary 1944

Deep in the lonely stillness of the night,
Amid the ruins of this war-scarred town,
I lie awake, and wish me far away,
Sharing the joys which you and I have known.

Naught now remains here for me, but to dream,
And live again those hours, when each to each,
Spoke in the language of our new-found love,
Unuttered thoughts that lay too deep for speech.

Strong is my hunger for thee, and how long,
Linger the hours apart from thee, and yet
Were we two parted for a myriad years,
Ne'er would I cease to love thee, nor forget.

Could I have but one wish, one hope fulfilled,
One dream to cherish, one desire to hold,
'Twere this – that future years may still enrich,
And mellow the remembrance of the old.

Experienced joys are sweet, but the, as yet
Untrodden road of love that lies ahead,
Holds promise of fulfilment of those hopes,
On which my hours of loneliness have fed.

So shall I pledge anew to thee my heart,
In expectation of requited love,
And vow to prize that which I seek of thee,
Throughout eternity, all else above.

Ciney, Belgium, 17th October 1944

A Moonlight Ramble

Silence and peacefulness,
    With hardly a breath or sigh,
And every leaf a-whispering to its mate
    As I pass by.

Moonlight and loveliness,
    And every ray a gem,
Each silvery beam a-shimmering on the lake
    A-down the glen.

Starlight and fantasy,
    With every star afire,
And wind-swept clouds a-prancing neath the blaze
    To rouse its ire.

Silence and peacefulness,
    With hardly a breath or sigh,
And every leaf a-whispering to its mate
    As I pass by.

Helvoirt, Holland, 3rd December 1944

Chrysanthemum

In Marrene, there's a spot where, 'mid snowy white bowers,
Chrysanthemums bloom in the wintery shade,
And there 'mid the last of the autumnal flowers,
Grow emblems of life, the Almighty hath made.

With envy I view thee, pure virginal flower,
That modestly bare thy sweet face to the day,
Designed yet to grace Flora's beauteous bower,
Anon when earth's glory hath faded away.

From out of thy heart sweet miss Innocence blushes,
The source of her beauty I fain would espy,
In confusion she flutters her maidenly tresses,
Her beauty to hide from my curious eye.

Thy life speaks of love which we men have forgotten,
Thy face has the stamp of a pattern divine,
The faith which in men has grown putrid and rotten.
Lends lustre and life to these petals of thine.

Alas that to die is thy fate sweetest flower,
So short is thy life, few the hours that fleet,
Fond lesson of life, since each day makes me older,
Should I not while young make some life doubly sweet.

The Gardener of heaven needs beautiful flowers,
And visits the earth seeking flowers to adorn,
The shrine wherein angels beguile away hours,
Reciting their matins to herald each morn.

When my glory is done, may I e'en like this flower,
Be borne by the Gardener of life, to the glen,
Where the flowers of His choice bloom unfading forever,
Eternally watching the drama of men.

Marrene, Belgium, 3rd January 1945

In Memory of Lieut. Eric Jones, Newcastle Emlyn, Killed in the Ardennes, Jan. 1945

Tread softly, yonder consecrated mound,
Hides in its earthy tomb a noble soul.
Stifle thy fevered pulse my heart, unroll
In friendship's tears thy grief this grave around.

Peaceful his life, let no unseemly sound,
In death his feelings stir. On glory's scroll,
His honoured name in worthy terms extol,
That we his steps may trace through hallowed ground.

Mark well the path whereon his feet were bent,
Peace for the oppressed of the earth he sought,
Duty the keynote of his life well-spent,
Selfless in aim the final deed he wrought.

God has reclaimed, but what in trust he lent,
That he, life's crown might gain, who nobly fought.

Luxemburg, 18th January 1945

Peace

Come Peace,
Elusive mistress of the joys of life,
Gather the threads of broken hearts that yearn
And hunger for thee, ere their cry is lost
In this world's strife.

And Peace
If thou hast aught of love for such as I,
Who am not worthy to be known of thee,
Come now in haste, the flame of hope grows dim
As years pass by.

For Peace,
Thy home is still the broken heart of man,
Despite the fools, despite the warlords, who,
Destined to run life's race with sword in hand,
Fell as they ran.

Grant Peace,
That all the loss, the bitterness, the pain,
Shall not leave thee unmoved, nor leave thee cold,
That they who gave their lives to woe thy hand,
Died not in vain.

Rise Peace,
Above the darkness of our man-made night,
Point out the way whereby the foot of man,
May tread again the way which leads to Him who said,
"Let there be light".

Then Peace,
When all the shoutings and the tumults die,
When hate and envy are despised of men,
Then shall the nations of the earth rejoice
That thou art nigh.

Bleckede, Germany, 15th June 1945

To My Son

A tale of war I'll tell you son,
Of the might of English Arms,
Of the valour of our country men,
Of a comradeship that warms.

While all the world looked on son
As the Gentiles did of old,
At the sight of the English David,
And the Bosche Goliath bold.

From northern shires we came son,
From south and east and west,
With a will to fight for right son,
And our spirit of the best,

And deep in the still of a warm June night,
The sea like our own mill pond,
We sailed away from our homeland,
Away to the great beyond.

And as we left old England's shores,
'Twas many a tear we shed,
For thoughts of home were dear son,
When love's last word was said,

For two whole days we sailed away,
And oft we searched the sky,
Seeking the dreaded Luftwaffe
And the shrill dive-bomber's cry,

But the butchers of Warsaw came not,
Nor the wolves of Rotterdam,
For the hand of God lay there twixt us,
And the terror of the Hun.

Then on the third day out son,
We saw the coast of France,
And to the Arromanches beach
Our troopships made advance.

And knowing not what lay before,
Nor yet our strength behind,
Onward we went in ignorance of
The hell we were to find.

And many a fight we fought son,
And many a battle won,
Till many a town in Normandy
Was ridden of the Hun.

Ere many weeks were passed son,
Our strength was tried full sore,
For naught but ruin lay behind,
And the Nazi hell before,

And the threat of death lay heavy son,
As many a comrade fell,
With seldom a decent burial,
And never a funeral knell,

But as our troops fought onward,
With guns all spitting death,
The teuton strength lay broken,
On many a Norman heath.

Our fame went forth before us,
And many a well-laid plan,
Of German brain was stemmed son,
By the gallant Englishman.

'Gainst heavy odds we fought son,
And many a time and oft,
Men jumped from blazing tanks, and fought
To keep their flags aloft,

Till the French regained their freedom,
And France again was free,
And the beaten foe reeled backward
To the shore of the Zuider Zee.

And there he paused to lick his wounds,
By the better soldiers shamed,
And sought yet to retain his strength
Ere hope of victory waned,

But mighty were our forces son,
And his brain could not conceive,
A plan to stem the advancing tide,
Continuing to achieve,

Great victories upon his men,
While each day brought anew,
Bad tidings from the Fatherland,
Where dark forebodings grew,

Well-nigh into hysteria son,
As allied airborne might,
Wrought havoc on their life by day,
And on their sleep by night.

Our soldiers halted not son,
While hot on the German heel
We pressed, nor ceased from fighting
In our chariots of steel.

And though the cost was heavy son,
At the bark of German guns,
Our faith was strong that God would bless
The efforts of his sons.

And the German eagle reeled and fell,
And his schemes were all undone,
And away he flew, nor stopped until
He reached his own hearthstone,

And there, with little more to lose,
And everything to gain,
He stood at bay, defiant still,
On the Hanoverian plain.

This was no time to halt son,
Now that the die was cast,
For he who hoped to rule the world,
Lay near defeat at last,

And fast and furious went the chase,
As his defences fell,
When allied soldiers stormed the might
Of the Nazi citadel.

'Twas thus the war was won my son,
That little boys like you,
Might live the life they might have lived,
Who gave their all for you,

So when you say your prayers son,
Tonight at mammy's knee,
Ask God to make you good
That you may worthy of them be.

Ibbenburren, Germany, 12th August 1945

A Ballad of Wester Kappeln

In the village of Wester Kappeln,
By the sign of the Sergeants' Mess,
There dwelt a fratting fraulein,
Whom we nicknamed 'Black Bess'.
Of the deeds of this fair lady,
This belle of a one-eyed town,
I've heard men speak in NAAFI bars,
From here to Munster Town.
They speak of it in Osnabruck,
In the street of Who Drunk Schnapps,
Of how old Bessie laid her net
And how she set her traps,
And nightly, sundry troops were caught
In the meshes of her net,
They say she did it all for love,
Not for the fags she'd get.
Her fame went out before her,
And competitors were keen,
Men couldn't live on bread alone,
If you get what I mean.
This village was so *klein*
And the frauleins were *nicht fel*
The troops could not be choosy
Though the lady might be stale.
They couldn't chose; it was a case
Of grab it while you can,
And Bess knew well that even a crust
Looks good to a starving man.
Of facial beauty had she none,
Of figure but a little,

Yet many goodly tunes have come
Out of a battered fiddle.
And though to frat with German girls
Was then strictly *verboten*
Old Bessie saw to it each night
Her door was *nicht geschlossen*.
Then fate it came and intervened
In the form of fleas and bugs,
'Twas found that troops who'd been with Bess
Had pimples on their lugs,
And though men felt to frat with Bess
Was good for their morale
They scorned the thought that they might get
A 'buggy' for a pal.
So poor old Bess was forced to move
By Regimental Orders
And now we're left with no one else
Susceptible to callers.
I've heard men say she spends her nights,
Seeking newer quarry
I hope she's been decarbonised
Or somebody'll be sorry.

Wester Kappeln, Germany, 10th August 1945

Little Man, What Now?

Lo, now there comes the aftermath of war,
The peace, the treaties, and the victor's sway,
While you debate the future of your world,
Seeking a peace to last beyond your day.

When last the chance was given you to build,
A new Jerusalem out of the old,
The vision of your youth was unfulfilled,
The knell of many cherished hopes was tolled.

The louder clamourings of the mob o'ercame
The nobler counsels of your inner self,
And tooth for tooth became your new-found creed,
And war for justice – peace for fame and self.

Your brave new world became an old man's dream,
Your Armistice – a citadel on sand,
Versailles – the breeding ground whereon the spawn
Of future wars waxed fat in every land.

Peace scorns the righteous wrath of outraged right,
Love for your fellow man, and this alone,
Must bear your torch, and form the bastion which,
Will stay the tottering pillars of your home.

Peace comes not, save at the call of love.
I would that this were known from pole to pole,
That friendship is the balm, which yet will prove
The healing of this planet's wounded soul.

God grant that same spirit which once made,
England a refuge to earth's outcast strays,
May through you, in this breathing space from war,
Lead earth's tired peoples in God's chosen ways.

Wester Kappeln, Germany, 8th August 1945

Nelly

Oh the years that were wasted, ere first I knew you,
Nelly my girl, my girl.
Oh the joy of the first lover's hour we knew,
Nelly my girl, my girl.
Endless the hours since we parted,
Yet my thoughts are always of you,
And even in dreams you are always before me,
Nelly my girl, my girl.

The flame that was lit by you in my heart,
Still burns for you, Nelly my girl,
And our parting has served but to heighten the flame
That consumes me, Nelly my girl,
The birds are all whispering your name in the twilight
Now that I walk alone,
And what shall I tell them, now you are not with me,
Nelly my own, my own.

How well I remember the hours we spent
Together, Nelly my girl,
And ever the chord of remembrance has wrung
The heart of me, Nelly my girl.
What would I not give to retrieve but one hour
Spent of an evening with you,
For the key to the door of this life's greatest gift,
Lies for me Nelly with you.

Ibbenburren, Germany, 15th October 1945

Captain Thorne, HQ Squadron

The time has come my friends to speak,
Of those grand days that used to be,
When A2 Echelon 'dug' its way
From France right into Germany.
And of the leaders of that crowd,
One stood alone above the mob,
Known to his friends and foes alike,
As Second IC, Captain Bob.

No great, outstanding traits had he,
Except perhaps, an uncurbed tongue,
Which scarcely ever seemed to cease
To wag from dawn till setting sun,
But when an organising mind
Was needed by the powers that be,
They always called on Captain Bob,
For none could plan as well as he.

And when a job was given him,
He scarcely ever seemed at sea,
He merely bit his fingernails,
And scratched his head haphazardly,
And then he'd give his orders out –
How this or that thing should be done,
And by the time his speech was o'er
He'd be right back where he'd begun.

There was no snobbery in him,
You could approach him any day,
No regimental touch for Bob,
He'd let a fellow have his say,
And if a chap had cause to grouse,
He only had to go and see,
To have it remedied at once
By Captain Bob, Second IC.

Somehow, I think his ancestors
Had miners in the family tree,
For when it came to digging holes,
No man could dig as deep as he.
I heard in France, he had a plan
Which only Bob could have laid on,
To dig beneath the Maginot Line
And join the Russians on the Don.

He had a soft spot for the girls,
Did this old Soldier, Captain Bob,
But, somehow, Robert never seemed to be
Successful on the job.
Yet if ability to drink
More than is normal marks a man,
Then here we had a man indeed,
For he'd out-drink a watering-can.

I hope he will not take amiss,
These little quips I've made tonight,
I'd rather rag him to his face,
Than do it when he's out of sight.
I'm sure I speak for everyone,
Who came to know him at his job,
That though they may forget all else,
They'll all remember Captain Bob.

Ibbenburren, Germany, 8th November 1945

Behold, The Man

No kingly pomp was present when, to earth,
He came to us, a babe born in manger,
We ridiculed His claim to be our Saviour,
And failed to reconcile God with His birth.
His words we scoffed at with sarcastic mirth,
And when to teach of God, He courted danger,
We called Him liar, hypocrite, blasphemer,
And in our ignorance, denounced His worth.
When in His agony, for drink he cried,
With vinegar, His parched mouth we filled,
And when to save our souls He would have died,
We nailed Him to a cross, and thereby killed
The voice of Him, who with His last breath sighed,
"Father, forgive them," ere His tongue was stilled.

Ibbenburren, Germany, Christmas 1945

Above Costozza

Here on this rocky mountain height, which holds
Its mighty arms athwart Costozza's brow,
I sit and watch the valley mists enfold,
The busy ploughman toiling down below.

Ah, with what wondrous patience doth he lead,
His weary oxen through the furrowed tracks,
And with what understanding do they heed,
The guide-ropes pressure on their heaving backs.

Content is he to do the appointed task –
The preparation for the future yield,
He leaves the rest to God, he does not ask,
Nor doubt that in good time, this furrowed field,

Will bring forth sustenance in wheat and grain,
Whose life lies dormant in the heavy soil,
And fill to overflowing once again,
His granaries in payment for his toil.

His the fulfilment of the written word –
That faith and patience have their own reward.

Costozza, Italy, 15th February 1946

Dear Dad (or The Fatigue Squad)

Send me a pick and a shovel Dad,
Send me a ball and chain,
I'm off to Grisignano,
To quarry stones again.
You who have toiled in the mines Dad,
By the sweat of your gleaming brow,
Will grieve to learn that your daily drudge,
Has become my portion now.

Thus do I serve my country Dad,
Now my fighting days are o'er
This is the fruit of the sacrifice
Of the men who've gone before,
That I, who am left must toil afresh,
While the giggling Eyeties stare
At the British lion's slaving cub
On Grisignano Square.

The keen young lads who'll follow me Dad,
Won't appreciate the worth
Of the toil that went to the making of
This drill square at its birth.
Little I thought I should ever crave
For the raging battle's din,
But compared to this, 'twas a labour of love
For your fed up offspring, Wyn.

Grisignano, Italy, 16th March 1946

Sergeant Major

He reigns supreme upon the barrack square,
Let troopers who dispute his rule beware,

His voice comes forth in great stertorous waves,
Reverberating through Costozza's caves.

He shouts aloud when whispers would suffice,
And stalks his men, just as a cat doth mice,

He issues regulations by the score,
And would-be Sergeant majors add some more,

And when men disobey his rules, he goes
And plays the devil with his NCO's.

Erect he walks, nor looks to left or right,
His belt with toothpaste powder gleaming white,

And awestruck Eyeties on Costozza's steep,
Gaze on this apparition just like sheep.

Few friends he hath, this is the price he pays,
For hounding men throughout his army days,

For with a Hitlerite technique, he stands
No disobedience of his shrill commands.

Yet I could envy him the happy fate,
Which has befallen him down here of late,

For some sweet senorita in Padova
Has dubbed old tartar, 'Panzer Cassanova'.

Costozza, Italy, 22nd March 1946

Glory

Deem it not glory if its quest should make,
Another's quest abhorrent unto thee,
True glory knows no favourites, but leaves
All men to seek its hideout patiently.

Practice forbearance as a noble art,
And scorn impatience as unworthy thee,
Make love thy sword, and tolerance thy shield
To storm the gates of immortality.

Condemn no man, for all have fallen short
Of that perfected state the gods have wrought.
And conquest of thy neighbour gives to thee,
No lordship o'er the glory which he sought.

The road to glory will be strewn with hopes,
Of those who tried through war the earth to own,
And sought their glory thus – forgetting that
Death waits their reaping, who but death have sown.

He who sets out to conquer all the world,
And makes himself the judge of his own deeds,
Begets no glory, but that short-lived fame
Which kills the selfsame ego that it feeds.

Count then those earthly conquests all as nought,
That are not moral conquests over self.
The only battle which true glory earns
Is that which man must fight against himself.

Refuse all substitutes the world may try,
To thrust upon thee, ere thy task is done,
Lose not the sight of this one, worthwhile aim
Whose prize is certain as tomorrow's sun.

This is the lasting glory, which no man
Can give to thee, and no man take away.
This is the conquest, that will carve thy name
On glory's scroll when thou has had thy day.

Costozza, Italy, April 1946

To 'Dally' the Canteen Girl

Who has a smile for every guy?
To please the vain and charm the shy,
Who even makes sophisticated sergeants sigh?
But Dally, the canteen girl.

She's but five feet four, and looks a mite
In her khaki slacks – a charming sight,
She makes up in charm what she lacks in height
Does Dally, the canteen girl.

The way she drives that great big truck,
For a slick gear change she's never stuck,
She has more than her share of female pluck
Has Dally, the canteen girl.

To some, she's a combination rare
Of sea-blue eyes, and cornflower hair,
But to me, she's a breath of English air
Is Dally, the canteen girl.

And I hope one day my sister Sue,
Whom I left way back in '42
Will grow to be like the girl I knew
As Dally, the canteen girl.

Costozza, Italy, 7th April 1946

The Victory Parade, Trieste

In the skies of Yugoslavia, lo a new star gleams,
And a newly risen Caesar indulges in his dreams,

And his dreams are all of conquest, as he views with eager eyes,
The war-scarred weakened Europe which around about him lies.

Tito's proven warriors are straining at the leash,
As they see the wealth and riches lying just beyond their reach.

They have fed upon the doctrine of the promise they have heard
From the mouth of their great leader, who has preached to them
this word –

"Worldly power is to the mighty, and the battle to the strong,
And the riches of this planet to the strongest states belong"

Statesmen of the four great powers have met in gay Paree
To safeguard the territorial rights of beaten Italy,

While they aim in this their meeting to preserve the status quo
In the region lying eastward of the valley of the Po.

There are nightly demonstrations in the Adriatic port,
And the followers of Tito wait our coming to report,

On the token force of allied arms now lying in the bay,
Making ready for the long awaited second day of May.

Battle-scarred Cruisers are anchored in the docks,
(Tito's troops are watching in the sun-scorched rocks)

World-famous Infantry, smart in khaki drill,
(Tito's troops are digging on the rock-strewn hill)

Tank tracks grating on the cobble-stoned street,
To the wonder of the populace and cheers of the fleet.

Scotch kilts swaying to the rumble of the drum,
And the blare of Yankee Tubas, as down the road they come.

Swiftly flying Mustangs diving in salute,
And cheeky little Auster planes, following in suit,

Chromium-plated 'Arty' Guns, gleaming in the sun,
And America's 'Blue Devil' men, marching at the run.

Multi coloured banners, pregnant with disdain,
Of any would-be victor, who dare challenge them again,

Skirl of the bagpipes in the sun-baked street,
Beating out their tempo to the marching feet,

And the tongues of Tito's demonstrators lose their cry,
As they realise their impotence when tanks pass by.

Night steals its way across the Adriatic sea,
Thoughtfully men make for home in troubled Italy,

The great parade of token allied armoured might is o'er,
And torch-lit nightly demonstrations now are seen no more,

And men go home to dream again their puny little dreams,
And dwell upon the wonders of a thousand might-have-beens,

And deep in Yugoslavia, in the great Danubian plain,
A new Dictator sits him down, and learns to think again.

Trieste, Italy, 2nd May 1946

To a Nightingale (Heard at Monte Galda, Italy)

The day is not for thee, only the night
Affords the silence that thou dost demand,
In awed expectancy, here I await,
The prelude to thy song, majestic, grand.

Like some lone Crusoe's on a desert isle,
Thy voice will come, and none shall challenge thee,
The night is still, and lo the stage is set,
Begin sweet bird thy cloying melody.

The clouds their curtains now have opened wide
To flood with light from out the crescent moon,
The stage on which thou wilt perform tonight;
The world's thy stage – it waits for thee alone.

Ah! Now I hear thee; from afar there come,
A haunting tune upon the midnight breeze,
Whose notes no minstrel in the world could form,
No human voice ere sang such notes as these.

Sad is thy lay tonight. Dost thou in song,
Bemoan the serfdom of this alien land,
Where wealth and poverty dwell side by side,
And want and husbandry go hand in hand?

Or maybe thou hast wandered from thy home,
Like unto me, and longst for bygone days,
When all was happiness, and not a tear
Bemarred the even tenor of thy ways.

It matters not – sing on, the dawn too soon
Will ring the curtain on thy mystic tune.

Monte Galda, Italy, May 1946

Squadron Leaders, Past & Present (2)

Major Reed, MC

Many a man has been noted,
For brilliance in ethical climes,
And many a man by his daring has won,
The esteem and applause of his times.
But my topic tonight is quite different,
And defying all army red tape,
I'll risk thirty days in the klink to reveal
The tale of the man with the cape.

No matter wherever we met him,
In the office or out on parade,
His battered gas-cape he'd be wearing
Like some relic of Turpin's decade.
But where lesser men would have feared
The quips of his officer mates,
No self-conscious qualms ever shook him,
Nor feared he the smirks of the fates.

I've heard it being said that at leave time,
To Surrey the Major would go,
But his gas-cape would always go with him,
He'd feel naked were it not so.
His batman had definite orders,
When laying his clothes for the day,
To see that the old cape was handy,
And he dare not do less than obey.

You'll agree that it must have been galling,
For Green, who is so spick and span,
After spending long hours a-batting
And doing his best for his man,
To see the wee Major while dressing,
With trousers and coat neatly pressed
Go and cover the lot with his gas-cape,
'Twould make any batman depressed.

When lecturing Troopers on tactics,
And speaking of Germans they'd meet,
The 'Bosche' was his word, never 'Jerry',
And he spat out the word with some heat,
But the things we invariably laughed at
On occasions like these when he spoke,
Were his cape, and his blinkin great map-board,
But he never quite saw through the joke.

Still all joking apart, let's give honour,
Where honour is due to the brave,
For this Major whose fashions I laughed at,
Sent many a Bosche to his grave,
Could I chose from a dozen new leaders,
I could wish for none better than he,
For 'tis men of his kind who bring nearer,
The dawn of the peace to be.

Bury St. Edmunds, June 1946

To My Bed

Ah sweet little bed, how proud though must be,
That an RSM should photograph thee,

'Tis a shame methinks that though shouldst be
The unwitting cause of controversy.

Diverse 'crowns' and multiple 'pips'
Have lain in peace on thy shapely hips,

Not even the bed where Diana lay,
Caused such a to-do in the Greek's heyday,

And never before have men been led
To curse the sight of their lowly bed.

Time was when though wast only meant
To be lain upon by the weary pent,

But time moves on, and now I find,
Thy role is the whim of a mastermind.

'Tis a scandalous shame that thy framework stout,
Should be made a stand for a kit lay out

And thy pillow soft meant for my head
Should be made to hold my pack instead.

The paraphernalia, and rigmarole
Of a soldier's kit have taken toll,

Of those graceful lines, which invited me
To spend long hours in thy company

Farewell my friend, for thou hast lost
That appealing mien, which charmed me most,

And thou hast become an excuse – a cause
For adding some more to existing laws.

And for thy disgrace, I owe my thanks
To an RSM of the 'Royal Tanks'.

Venice, Italy, 16th June 1946

The Prisoner of Buchenwald

Be not afraid, for even I,
Am human too like unto thee,
Let not surprise at this my state,
Repel thou who has made me free.
Oft in my tortured dreams I've prayed,
That for me soon the day would dawn,
When I'd be free again to see
The little town where I was born,
But lone confinement now has wrought
Its havoc on my weakened frame,
And things that once I valued much,
Henceforth will never be the same.
Weak, palsied creature that I am,
Who would know me as of yore?
My hair grown prematurely grey
At sights undreamt in ancient lore
Full five and twenty men once lived,
Within this foul and confined space,
Where scarce a ray of Heaven's sun
Could shed its light upon my face,
Despised, poor, forgotten men,
Whose only crime was this – that we
Had dared to raise our voice
Against a tyrant of man's liberty.
For this, I gave my life in pawn,
And thought it right that I should speak,
When freedom, which I loved so much,
Was held as being of the weak
And foolish hauntings of the mind
Of those who had no greater aim

In life than but to cherish some
Utopian dream – bereft of fame.
My loved ones were my life to me,
Nor loved I worldly fame or self,
I have no dreams of world renown,
But cherished freedom for itself,
And for my faith and firm belief,
In the inherent good in man,
I found myself within this cell,
Wherein a living death began,
To wreak its scars upon my life,
And made at times my mind to doubt,
The wisdom of my stand against
The forces hemming me about.
These four grey walls, so cold and damp,
Have been the only things whereon,
My eyes were ever wont to stray,
From break of dawn till setting sun.
In endless darkness gazed upon,
Their clammy greyness day by day,
I but imagined them to be
From this foul bed whereon I lay.
When first the grim herald of death,
Paid his grim visit to my cell,
He took away my dearest friend,
None other loved I half as well,
His death was as the passing of
A wave, upon an endless sea,
Unsung, his sacrifice upon
The alter of man's liberty.
They dug a hole there where my chain,

Lies fastened to the prison floor,
And there they laid him, he, whose death
But added to the cross I bore.
No more could we who now were left,
Creep to and fro within this room,
Lest we should in the darkness tread
Upon and desecrate his tomb.
And thus we tarried day by day,
And daily some would slowly die,
Until at last there but remained,
No other prisoner here but I.
When tortured limbs grew cold in death,
I could not pity them not I,
For I was in the self-same plight,
Believing too, I soon must die,
And thus I hardened all the more
My heart, that when my hour would be,
I would be ready at the last
To pay death's price for liberty.
So slow the days were wont to pass,
And each day longer than the last,
Wherein my mind sought its repose,
In dim remembrance of things past,
And thus I started thinking of
The circumstances which had led,
To my imprisonment, and that
Of twenty-four, who now were dead.
Forgive me if I speak my mind,
My heart is bitter that I know,
The price that my convictions claimed
Of me in suffering and woe,

Will all have been in vain, if I
Fail in my self-appointed task
Of saying this while I have breath,
List' to my words is all I ask.
The world that stands so idly by,
While tyrants rule with sword and rod,
And thus give them the chance to thrive,
Are guilty in the eyes of God,
For it is they who thus create,
The soil wherein the seed of wrong,
Will germinate, and overthrow
The plant of righteousness ere long.
So go you back – I cannot take,
The liberty you offer me,
The few, short days I now have left,
I'd as soon spend in slavery,
But take you to your fellow men
This message that I give to you,
That they may learn from this my word,
And, please God, profit from it too,
That peace and love can never be
While men still close their eyes to sin,
Nor harken to the still small voice
Of conscience calling from within,
And when men think of Buchenwald,
May they remember this my word –
That freedom to do wrong, unchecked
Leads but to terror, and the sword.

Palmanova, Italy, 8th July 1946

The London Victory Parade

Honour the brave and the living,
Long may their glory shine,

Your sons have returned to your keeping,
But God has taken mine.

Sad and alone he left me,
But I could not say him nay,

And he gave his life for the victory
We celebrate today.

This is a sight to be proud of
As your sons go marching by,

But prouder am I, remembering
The one who had to die,

And a thousand hearts are bursting
To convey their heartfelt thanks

My heart lies there in the unfilled gap
Within the marching ranks.

Your sons salute their ruler
As the sound of the trumpet rings,

Mine salutes in glory
Besides the King of Kings.

I like to think that somewhere,
Up there in the Heaven's blue

They are rejoicing with us,
And my son is with them too,

And I can hear the voices
Of angel choirs free,

Singing the joyful anthem,
'To God the Victory'.

And I have ceased to worry,
That he is sad like me,

For he went on to glory
In goodly company.

For marching with him, side by side
Are Paddy Finucane

And Rennie of the Fifty-first
And Wingate of 'Chindit' fame.

And Roosevelt marches with them,
And he's smiling as of yore,

For his long infirmity is passed,
And he needs his stick no more.

And there's Jock Campbell swinging,
In stride with 'Straffer Gott'

And all are counted equals
Before the eyes of God.

For, unlike us who glory
In personal triumphs won,

They know that for this victory
We owe our thanks to One.

For none are indispensable
To the cause of worldly peace,

Save He, who rides upon the storm,
And bids its tumult cease.

So let your thanks be unto Him,
That your sons are home again,

Give Him the power and glory,
For evermore, Amen.

London, 6th June 1946

Churchill

Forget him never, for he was the rock,
To which we clung, when all our hope seemed lost.
Deny him not the glory, neither mock
This last of the Elizabethan host.

Like unto John the Baptist, known of old,
His was a voice from out the wilderness,
Which sought to rouse our conscience as he told,
Prophetic words of German beastliness.

Born out of greatness, nurtured in the strength
That came from faith in his own destiny,
His was the hand that led us through the length
Of that hard road which led to victory.

Thankless his task. Let history abhor
The ungrateful voice that bade his rule to cease,
And called the candour he had shown in war,
His studied insolence in days of peace.

This was our leader. Did he not evoke
The inherent greatness of our island race?
Yet we with one swift, unexpected stroke,
Denied to him the honours of the chase.

Why is it that those days by war accursed,
Revealed our nation's insight at its best,
While that same quality is at its worst,
Now that the peace has brought us hard-earned rest.

But should a day of retribution fall,
And England once again be found at bay,
The people who forgot him will recall,
The leader they dethroned but yesterday.

London, 6th June 1946

To My Boots

Poor objects of pity,
Spat on and brushed,
Thy squeaky objections
Cruelly hushed,
Lying in idleness
Here on my bed,
No more with thine owner
Life's byways to tread.
Heeltips all polished,
And toecaps right-dressed,
Pampered like children,
And likewise caressed,
Sad must thy feelings be,
Now that the lads,
Have curtailed thy freedom
Thou victim of fads.
Oft have I honed thee
With toothbrush and comb,
To outshine the gems
In Tuttankhamen's tomb,
Once thou didst lead me
Through fire and shell,
While others around me
Faltered and fell,
Yet thou wast happy
For thou wast well-fed,
With juices of Dubbin,
Green coloured and red.
Well thou didst serve,
But thy service is done,

Yet I repay thee
With nourishment none,
Needs must thou suffer
In silence today,
I have my orders,
And must obey,
Mine not to reason
That leather, unfed
Rots like a canker
And soon will be dead.
Shine on my beauties,
Though numbered thy days,
To please Squadron Leaders
And merit their praise.
And when they, whose orders
Thy life did abuse
To please sundry whims
At the cost of thy use
Will find that when rain comes,
Thy value is nil,
They can but blame themselves,
Though I doubt if they will.

Palmanova, Italy, 4th July 1946

Rocky Knight

In the training camp at 'Bovy',
There resides a chap called Rocky,
Who was once a Sergeant Mech. In this 'ere shower,
Just a typical old sweat,
With a face so grimly set,
That it seemed to ooze authority and power.

On the 'Rockies' of this crowd,
(In his length of service proud)
He would gaze with calm disdain as on a worm,
For he'd memories galore,
Of those grand old days of yore,
When he'd fought with Bonny Charles at Bannockburn.

And his brain was stocked with jokes,
Of those Pukha Sahib blokes,
Who had crossed his path way back in ninety-four,
And he never seemed to tire,
Spinning yarns around the fire,
While we chaps who listened craved for more and more.

He possessed that skill so rare,
Of telling lies with such great care,
That his audience was convinced he spoke the truth,
He could tell the greatest 'stinker'
With an eye which made each listener
Think of Rocky as a second Bramwell Booth.

He had such convincing ways,
That throughout his army days,
He could bluff his way thorough any kind of danger,
And his bluffs were so well planned,
That had he wished to try his hand,
I believe he could have got away with murder.

In the concerts we once had,
When army life was not too bad,
He would play to spellbound audiences each night,
And his acting as Salome
In the concert at Bleckede,
Gave posterity the fame of Rocky Knight.

To the girls who love at sight,
He was known as 'Toothless Knight'
And the fame of his technique reached to Nanking,
Though he looked like 'Mad Garoo'
Rocky knew a thing or two,
For no woman ever had him on a string.

All his loves were short-lived epics,
Both at home and in the tropics,
And the colour bar ne'er troubled him a bit,
He could love with equal ardour,
In a field as in a parlour,
And he never seemed to fail to score a hit.

When the moon was shining bright,
And the wolves would roam at night,
In the troglodytian caves of old Costozza,
Scores of Senoritas fair
(Some with garlic in their hair)
Come to woo this hardboiled fitter Cassanova.

When my army days are o'er
And I'm back at home once more,
I shall look in vain for men like him in 'Blighty'
Though my demob day's in sight
I'd sign on, yes, so I might,
If I thought I'd come across some more like Rocky.

Palmanova, Italy, 10th August 1946

To Taffy Ryan on his Wedding

Sing a song of hope all day,
And God will surely hear it,
He will not grant you what you need,
Unless you ask Him for it.
Each human heart on this earth of His,
Has a Heavenly spark within it,
But the spark will never be a flame,
Unless you daily tend it.

This earth you're passing through is His,
 As much as the Heaven above it,
And your holy service to the Lord
Is the work you do while in it.
Though your heart may sin, and you may not feel,
That there is much good within it,
Remember God can make a saint of a soul
When the world has damned it.

Though the sky above be dull or blue,
The same Heaven lies beyond it,
And the blue of life is greater far
Than the cloud if you only seek it.
Though the tree may never touch the sun,
It tries its best to reach it,
And God records not what you've done,
But how well you tried to do it.

The road of life is a one-way street,
With many a hill upon it,
But there is no turning back for those
Who seek the goal beyond it.
May the goal you seek be the way to Heaven,
Each step bring you nearer to it,
May you hear the porter say, 'Well done'
When, at last, you enter through it.

Villach, Austria.

In Memory of Len Hill, Died Udine, Italy, August 1946

Hang low ye clouds, and shield his lowly head,
From burning heat of the Italian sun,
And when the day's oppressiveness is done,
Water with angel's tears his lonely bed.

Guard him from winter's tempests and its gales,
Ye hills that tower above Udine's plain,
Like to our hills at home, for we were twain
Born of the selfsame dam – beloved Wales.

Take earth thine own. He was but ours on trust.
That which thou givest thou dost take away.
Thou didst but lend him to us for a day,
His poor remains are thine – his dust, thy dust.

Cradle him in thy bosom earth, to die
Afar from home his fate in foreign land.
No mother at his deathbed held his hand,
To give him courage when the end was nigh.

Fame knew him not, and that elusive sprite
The world calls glory, heedless, passed him by.
Unmarked his passing, even as the sigh
Of falling leaves in an autumnal night.

Not for each man the centre of life's stage,
Whereon all men may view their worthy deeds,
But silent men there are, whom honour breeds,
And unrecorded, grace not history's page.

Of such as these was my departed friend,
Who, known of many, valued by a few,
In silence worked behind life's scenes, and drew
His joy from serving others to his end.

I'll think of him as each succeeding day,
Enhances realization of his worth.
That I, like him, when duty calls me forth
To serve my fellow mortal, may obey.

Villach, Austria, 30th August 1946

The Miner's Death

'Mid the stench of sweating bodies,
In an air-deficient hole,
He strove with nature daily
In a frenzied search for coal,
But fate, relentless, dogged his steps,
His fearless heart to woo,
Till in death he formed part of the clay,
Which in life he tunnelled through.

'Mid the sleepless night of the inner dark,
He toiled in a ghastly tomb,
With but a spark from his safety lamp
To relieve the outer gloom,
And I, his butty in the seam,
Am dumb with a speechless sorrow,
For the knell they toll for him today,
May be rung for me tomorrow.

"But what is it to me," says one,
"That a miner's wage is death
That he toils 'neath half a mile of earth
Each day with laboured breath?"
With life, my friend, he pays for coal,
Which the likes of you and me
Have used, and the world is poorer far
For the loss of such as he.

Know you no shame, all you who buy
With gold, what was hewn in blood,
Condemning men to earn their bread,
In squalor, filth and mud,
Have you no thought to spare for those,
Who are left behind to mourn,
Can you, unmoved, behold their tortured hearts
In anguish torn?

Yet I who grieve with bitter tears,
One consolation know,
That his soul lives on in a realm above,
Though his body rot below,
And he, who long in the darkness toiled,
Has won to a greater light,
For the fruit of the seed he sowed at dawn,
God reaps with the fall of night.

Whitland, 8th February 1947

In Memory of Alderman T L Phillips

Ye people who would serve your fellowman
Hark this man's passing, that his life may be
A true example of a life well spent
In serving others with integrity.

For five and twenty years he served, and yet
The laurels that were his, unbidden came,
He did not stoop to gain the applause of men,
But was content to earn an honest name.

He served no sect or creed. Conscience alone
Dictated to him what was false or true.
Nor did he strive at other people's cost
To please a favoured and selected few.

He knew the hardest taskmaster of all
The fickle public, who are prone to hold
Ideas which change with every passing tide
And scorn the wider vision of the old.

So many men set out as once he did,
To serve the common good at man's behest.
Yet many curb their aims but to fulfil
Those selfish policies which serve them best.

But here was one who strayed not from the path
Of honest service. One who tried each day,
In the vicissitudes of public life.
To be a man of honour, come what may.

And in this modern world, where honest men
Are at a premium, it were well that we
Should strive to emulate this man, who scourned
To trade his soul for popularity.

Whitland, 14th July 1947

Lines Written on the Occasion of the Wedding of G Williams & Eileen 'Clyde Bank'

The date of this tale I now relate
Was nineteen hundred and forty-eight,

Churchill's day of glory had fled,
And Atlee stood at the prow instead.

The world was weary of battles grim,
Of rationed foods and fashions trim,

And the yeomen of England thrived on chips,
In the glorious days of 'Austerity Cripps'.

Such was the state of our land, when down
By train there journeyed to Whitland town,

A lad, keyed up with ambition fine,
To fire a train on the railway line,

And maybe, someday, to drive alone,
A loco engine to Wittingbourne.

Tall was he with the loping gait,
Of a seasoned hunter of trophies great,

Neat and slim, and fit withal
To grace the floor of a Hunter's Ball.

No time had he for the appraising glance
Of the sloe-eyed girls at the Whitland dance,

For he was true to the moral code
Of the footplate men of the iron road,

His heart enslaved by the silvery gleam
Of a streamlined damsel, fed on steam.

Alas, for men with a one-track mind,
Who have but one love, and that love blind,

For the female species have but to frown
And man's castles in air come tumbling down.

Such was the end of this victim of fate,
In nineteen hundred and forty-eight,

For taking a stroll one summer's day,
Up a tortuous hill near 'Tiger Bay',

He spied through a hole where the bushes shrank,
The home of the carter, Jonah Clydebank.

And there at the gate stood gazing down
On this strapping laddie from Whitland town,

A comely damsel, and girls like she,
Have been known to affect stronger men than he.

She summed him up with her eagle eye,
Ere I ween a moment had yet passed by,

And she saw that the prize in her grasp was good,
For Cupid, the watchful, understood,

And he sped an arrow straight and true,
To the heart of this innocent Buckaroo,

And all his ambition to drive a train,
Was lost like the dust in the summer rain.

Great events have beginnings small,
And that is our story each and all,

For the seed of love that was sown that day,
Is bearing its fruit in this church today.

And ere my tale I bring to a close,
A fitting toast I would fain propose,

Long life and happiness ever and aye,
For this man and maid, and if I may,

I'll express the hope that this tale of mine,
In nineteen hundred and forty-nine,

May serve as a warning to men of dreams,
Who've no room for girls in their puny schemes.

And may they, like him, have cause to thank
The world for a wife like Eileen Clydebank.

Whitland, 1949

The Dairies' Pin-Up Girl

I dedicate these verses
To a heroine of note,
Who, if she stood for parliament,
Would surely get my vote,
Through her you earn your living,
Your debt is great I vow,
For where would your great factory be
If it wasn't for the cow?

The ladies in the office,
The damsels in the Lab,
The greasy transport Wallahs
And the boss, Louis Mcnab,
The condensary teenagers,
And your worthy engineers,
Owe more by far to cow-juice,
Than they'll repay in years.

Proud Leonard in his Wolsely
And Hill in his old Ford,
And all the big directors
Of the Milk Marketing Board.
Though they're so proud I'll warrant
They've not realised till now,
They owe their thanks for all their wealth
To the innocent old cow.

Down in the transport shanty,
Old Billa's at his work,
And Harold in his taxi
Looks like Kemmal Attaturk.
I've heard it said at bedtime,
They bend their knees and bow,
With pride and joy before the shrine
Of their pin-up girl, the cow.

So varied are the talents of
The creamery employees,
Old Ieuan smells a faulty churn
A mile away with ease.
He can't half poke his nose in
And yet he knows not how,
Such smells of rare distinction
Emanate from an old cow.

The condensary department
Are busy filling tins,
So ably led by Fred and Dan,
The terrible young twins.
At times down in their section,
There's such an awful row,
They curse the day inventors boxed
The products of the cow.

When enterprising farmers try
To increase monthly cheques,
By adding water to the milk,
They find such schemes are wrecks,
For Mair in the laboratory
Soon wrinkles up her brow,
When icicles start forming on
The milk from someone's cow.

Your drivers here are varied,
Some half-blind like poor old Ben,
Who bumped into a horse one day,
And swore it was a hen.
I nearly laughed my head off once,
It really was a 'wow'
To see him doff his cap, and say
"Good morning" to a cow.

The mayor of Cwmfelin,
Jack Ivor of renown,
Has promised me that one day,
Within this worthy town,
He'll cut from out an oak tree,
A sturdy, seasoned bow,
And carve there from a statue
To your pin-up girl, the cow.

Whitland, September 1951

To 'Benji the Post', Guest of Honour at the Whitland Angling Association Dinner

Now this is the tale of 'Benji the Post',
The pick of the bunch of this fishing host.

Known through the length and breadth of the land,
As the ace of the pack in the fisher band,

A man whose skill with the rod and line,
Is fitting fare for this tale of mine.

And like all fishing tales that ever were told,
I'll dispense with the truth, if I may be so bold.

Now the tale of his wonderful skill began,
Ere he reached the age of a full-fledged man,

In the days of his youth in the Abbey brook
Where a bent old pin was his only hook,

And his rod, a stick from the Abbey wood
Which he wielded as only old Benji could.

No trout was safe from his wonderful bait,
And the hours he kept were long and late,

And often the morning sun would rise,
Ere Benji reached home with his fisherman's prize.

Now he kept his bait in a frying pan,
Did Benjamin Evans the worrum man,

Fed on moss and codliver oil,
Soaked in a mixture of virgin soil,

Murphy the baliff was unknown then,
And nothing worried fisherman Ben,

For a day on the hay at the Abbey meant
That he could fish to his heart's content.

The fame of his skill swept far and wide,
On the springtime surge of the mating tide,

And trout who came up with the Severn Bore
Learnt to dodge the haunts of old Benji Soar.

Now sad was he no longer to feel,
The bulging weight of a well-stocked creel,

He worried and worried, and wondered when,
He would catch the elusive trout again.

And then, one day by the river shore
He met old John from the Maritime Store,

And John, as all his cronies know,
Could even catch trout with an arrow and bow,

He pittied Benji and strove to find
A way of helping a kindred mind,

And Benji, who wished to recoup his fame,
Stuck to John for the good of his name.

Now John, who was not averse to share,
And to help a man who was willing to dare,

From his store of knowledge concocted a brew,
Whose ingredients resembled an Irish stew,

Swedes and carrots and what have you,
All served as fare for this wonderful brew,

With peas from a lousy old salmon kite,
Forked in the Marlais at dead of night.

No witch's cauldron ever stank,
Like this message of John's so foul and rank,

But out of it all came a wonderful paste,
Whose smell was unequalled except for its taste.

And down to the Gronw with heart aflame,
Went Benji the Post to recoup his fame,

Carrying a pot, whose mysterious content
Betrayed a stink wherever he went.

And ere Ben had fitted his tackle on,
The trout got wind of the terrible pong,

And out on the bank they jumped with glee,
All bent on solving the mystery,

And Benji the Post just stood aghast,
Fumbling with rod, and struggling with cast,

While all around him, trout galore,
Breathed their last on the Gronw shore.

Years have passed since that wonderful day,
When he learnt to fish the poacher's way,

But days like those are gone for good,
Now Murphy the Bailiff stalks the wood.

Though he fishes, my friends, till his dying day,
Benji will be the first to say,

No bait on earth can compare with the stew,
That came to be called the Marine Stores Brew.

Whitland, 18th October 1952

Lines Written on the Occasion of the Wedding of Eddie Davies & Marion Morgan

Down in a street of great renown
In the busy centre of Whitland town,
There dwelt a man, whose graces rare
Were crowned by wealth of curly hair.

Full many a lass of hopeful mien,
Stealing a glance at this lad were seen,
But he had eyes for none but one
And she led him a race ere the goal was one.

He varied his talents and numerous too,
Like ingredients in an Irish stew.
And he had a tongue which none could gag,
This reporter ace of the local rag.

Every day, were it wet or fair,
He would hie him down to Narberth square,
And would there concoct some spicy brews
To serve as fare for "The Weekly News".

Yet this was but one of the talents fine,
Which brought such fame to this pal of mine,
For he had a way with a billiard cue,
Which brought envious stares from the motley crew

Who spent their evenings, six 'til ten,
Chasing a ball in the billiard den,
And he was the man who held the reins
On parish councillors playing Cain.

On unspecified topics of import great,
For none but he their tongues abate.
On summer nights his skill was seen,
As a batsman of note on the village green,

And I do not doubt that the same is true,
(Strictly in private, twixt me and you)
That he once hit a ball with a mighty slam
Which hit a young tart on a Swansea tram,

And 'twas only the skill of old 'W D'
Kept the case out of court, believe you me.

One redeeming point in this batman's rash,
Was the well-trained growth of his two inch tash.
Spread out one inch each side of his nose,
A specimen rare as a thornless rose.

'Tis strange that a man, whose abilities shone,
Like a comet of note in an age long gone,
Should have met with a girl who called his bluff,
And brought to his knees this hardboiled 'buff'.

To be caught in a net by this woman laid,
Yet is ever the way with a man and his maid,
That sooner or later the day will come
When a woman talks and the man stays dumb,

Ready to favour her slightest whim,
When her smallest wish is a law to him.
Caught like a trout in a fisher's net,
From which none has invented a way out yet.